OUT OF THE ASHES

WES BROUSSARD

Edited by **TAYLOR KELLIHER**

Illustrated by **BOBBY BARNHILL**

Foreword by **CHRIS THOMAS**

LAKEVIEW PUBLICATIONS

First Printing, 2020

ISBN: 9798597638928

Book Cover Design: BOBBY BARNHILL
Editing: TAYLOR KELLIHER
Publishing: LAKEVIEW PUBLICATIONS
Formatting: CRAIG A. PRICE
Forward: CHRIS THOMAS

CONTENTS

This book is dedicated to the incredible brothers and sisters at St. Mary's Missionary Baptist Church, with special attention to Brother Joe Lea, Brother June, Brother Stanley, and their pastor, Kyle Sylvester Senior.

FOREWORD

Chris Thomas

I do not know of anyone better qualified to write a book of this nature than Wes. His life has always been geared toward shining a light into the darkest of places. I have personally benefited from his gifting and friendship for over 12 years and cannot imagine where my life would be without his voice. He champions the broken, the lost, the confused, the overlooked; and in my case the arrogant and passionately misguided. As Wes focused on my strengths and gifts, it gave me courage and insight to work on my weaknesses.

Out of the Ashes is a book the world desperately needs right now. As a nation, we are searching for this light to shine brightly into our hearts, so it can highlight what needs to change. In this book, Wes shares an incredible story of an extremely hateful and violent crime that had the potential to leave a group of believers completely shattered. You will find on this journey, no matter what you are facing, God never leaves us hopeless. Regardless of the actions of those around us, God is always in power. We can never allow the actions of others to negatively change our hearts. To quote my favorite person in all of history, Dr. Martin Luther King, *"Let no man pull you low enough to hate him."*

Prepare yourself to be challenged to see people and your story differently. My prayer is that you would know, no matter what you are facing, you too can rise out of the ashes to find truth and wholeness.

SECTION ONE: WRESTLING WITH DOUBT

He has told you, O man, what is good; And what does the Lord require of you but to do justice, to love kindness, And to walk humbly with your God?

— MICAH 6:8 (NASB)

CHAPTER ONE

Helpless Revelation

The loneliest moment in someone's life is when they are watching their whole world fall apart, and all they can do is stare blankly.

— F. SCOTT FITZGERALD

IN APRIL OF 2019, I was playing on my phone in a theater in Lake Charles, Louisiana— oblivious to the turn my life was about to take. As I waited for the movie, *The Best of Enemies*, to start, I read an article about three historically black churches that had just been burned to the ground only a few days apart in central Louisiana (about an hour and a half away). I couldn't believe something so openly hateful was happening more than half a century removed from the heart of the Civil Rights Movement. Three houses of worship, each roughly 100 years old, the hub of life and spirituality in these small towns, were entirely incinerated. The effects would be deep and long-reaching, damaging race relations for decades. The term "Bombingham" came to mind (I'll explain more later). As my movie started, I prayed for the communities affected by this vicious, unspeakable crime and the unity of my beloved Louisiana.

The movie was about Ku Klux Klan klavern leader C. P. Ellis, a man with considerable political connections, who fought against school integration in 1970's Durham, North Carolina. His opponent was Anne Atwater, also known as Roughhouse Annie, who had brazenly served the disenfranchised black community all of her adult life. Throughout the film, we see the racist behavior typical of KKK members—violence, collusion, blackmail, sexual assault, etc. While I know featuring this God-awful evil is necessary to establish the characters and plot of the film, watching the vile acts remained difficult for me to stomach. Halfway through the film, we discover that C. P. Ellis has a child who is severely mentally handicap. The boy is his oldest son, still an important role in the South to this day. While this man is confident and savvy in his day-to-day dealings, when faced with the condition of his languishing child, he's utterly broken.

About halfway through the film, we are shown a meeting wherein C.P. Ellis is forced to meet face-to-face with members of the black community. During the meeting, one of his opponents, Howard Clement, starts to share that all parents are afraid when their children face the dangers of life. At this point, Ellis cuts in to say what he incorrectly presumed the black parent was about to add: we are all the same, because we all fear for our children. That being the case, there's no reason to be racist, right? Mr. Clement matter-of-factly corrected Mr. Ellis by stating black parents and children have the additional danger of violent racism to contend with, which is the chief concern of their community. He went on to add how desperately *helpless* each parent feels as they attempt to prepare their children for a world wherein their freedom, their dignity, and even their lives could be terminated without warning or just cause. It was this helplessness that dehumanized the black community, not just the evil actions and equally evil inactions of some of their white neighbors. At that moment, Ellis was rocked. He did know, unlike most white people, exactly what it meant to have a child who was wildly disadvantaged and how soul-wrenching it was to be entirely *helpless* to save him.

Shockingly, I was beginning to empathize with C.P.

Ellis! As a large white man, I'd never really had to suffer any kind of discrimination, but recent events in my life had left me feeling *helpless* in a way I didn't know was possible. The fear that fills the void when hope is lost can unhinge you in unexpected ways. In truth, I was reeling in my own life, barely clinging to God's love and goodness for survival. I was scared for my children and myself and felt entirely *helpless* to overcome the onslaught I was facing. Maybe there was more of Mr. Ellis in me than I thought: we are all only one catastrophe away from experiencing total helplessness.

CHAPTER TWO

New Tactics

I used to want to fix people, but now I just want to be with them.

— BOB GOFF

ANNE ATWATER WAS in the room during the aforementioned meeting with C.P. Ellis and Howard Clement. By providence, she knew about this man's broken child through the orderlies at the mental hospital where Ellis's son was a permanent resident. At that moment, she could have twisted the knife deeply into the soul of her sworn enemy, which would normally have given her a great deal of pleasure. In fact, over a forty-year period, Roughhouse

Annie routinely shared her hatred for C.P. Ellis. She even repeatedly admitted she wanted to kill the man by decapitation! In this moment, however, she chose to get her point across with grace. She waited until they were alone, spoke softly to the most shattered area of his life, and made sure he understood the connection between his most broken place and every minute of the lives lived by his black neighbors. There was no denying her insight or arguing against her logic, and they both knew it.

At first, the Klan man did what he could to refute her claims with shallow rhetoric and knee-jerk anger. Decades of disgust churned in him to dismiss the revelation of how much common ground he shared with people he saw as less than human. Nevertheless, in short order, he was unable to continue to do so. The grace and kindness of his opponents toward his ailing son and struggling family broke down his shabbily constructed walls of rage. Walls that crumbled once he realized how much he had in common with his black neighbors during the most vulnerable moments of his life. As this belligerent leader of ignorant men was struck by the plight of the black citizens of Durham, his perspective was powerfully changed. To dismiss their pain and helplessness was to dismiss his own, something he couldn't do.

I hate spoilers, so I will leave the incredible ending of this film alone for now. It is enough to say the movie was expertly crafted, highly enjoyable, and poignantly inspirational. It was yet another experience that provoked me to continue to seek racial reconciliation in my sphere of influence. That was where I left it, or so I thought. The next day, I concluded my business and headed back home to Prairieville, Louisiana, just south of Baton Rouge. On the way, I felt the leading of the Holy Spirit to visit the churches that were burned down. I was hesitant. The last thing I wanted to do was come across as some fly-by-night "white savior" who thinks he's earning a merit badge for showing up during a difficult time for the black community (commonly referred to as a "hood badge," even though the fires happened in a very rural area). After years of living and working in some of the most marginalized communities, in one of the most poverty-stricken states in this great country, I knew that approach would do more harm than good. Following the leading of the Holy Spirit can be a very sensitive matter, and I couldn't afford to be wrong on this one.

The fear that fills the void when hope is lost can unhinge you in unexpected ways.

— WES BROUSSARD

CHAPTER THREE

Showing Up

Courage starts with showing up and letting ourselves be seen.

— BRENÉ BROWN

I DIDN'T KNOW a soul in central Louisiana, or the first thing about the unique history of the people there. Plus, I had no way of connecting with anyone at the three churches, because the buildings no longer existed. I am an almost unbearably practical person, so those hurdles did loom in the forefront of my mind. That wasn't why I hesitated. The real reason for my trepidation was deeper than logistics: I couldn't stand the thought of being perceived as disingenuous. Not on this. Not during such a traumatic time. Even the idea makes me cry as I write this—people need unity, wisdom, and power to deal with these incredibly complex and inflammatory issues. How much more so when those people are reeling at the soul level. The last thing they need is shallow pandering. In my mind, shallow pandering is worse than indifference, and I see indifference as a particularly vile brand of privilege. I was afraid I wouldn't be able to overcome that label, and a little scared I deserved it.

Still, I couldn't get past his voice. I had first heard him speak to me just before my 18th birthday, piercingly clear and solid. At the time, I was so hateful. More of a new-ager in some ways, more of an agnostic in others. To make a long story short, I asked him, a God I didn't really believe in, why He would die such a gruesome death when He had the power to stop it. To my absolute amazement, He answered: *For you.* I was undone. My pain, anger, shame, and brokenness all crumbled in the presence of his sacrificial love. I couldn't speak—all I could do was weep. Those two words revolutionized my life back in February of 2001, but it wouldn't be the last time He spoke to me like that.

As I haggled over my decision in the parking lot of a random gas station somewhere just off of I-10, He challenged me directly: *You've wanted racial reconciliation since you were a child... are you going to pass on this opportunity? When all I'm asking you to do is show up?* Now, I'd like to make something very clear: I knew if He was sending me, I was going to have to do more than just "show up." Our showing up is typically the prerequisite for Him changing the world, because once He starts working on the hearts and minds of people, there's no telling where it will end. He wasn't asking for my attendance. He wanted my trust in Him to override my precious practicality and gnawing fears. As I gazed down the interstate, I knew that if I left right then, I'd still be able to beat Baton Rouge's gridlock traffic. In less than two hours, I'd be in the comfort of my home, not in the middle of some intrusive adventure with God. I sighed heavily, put my SUV in gear, and headed north for St. Landry Parish and the remains of those three incinerated churches. If there was even a chance He would provide an opportunity for me to serve these people, His children going through hell, who was I not to show up?

In my mind, shallow pandering is worse than indifference, and I see indifference as a particularly vile brand of privilege. I was afraid I wouldn't be able to overcome that label, and a little scared I deserved it.

— WES BROUSSARD

CHAPTER FOUR

Facing Death

Leaving the familiar for unknown terrain is like a death—and feeling this level of finality should snap one back to life for life has greater meaning in the face of death.

— DONNA LYNN HOPE

WHILE MOST OF us have felt like a square peg trying to fit into a round hole from time to time, the entire state of Louisiana is an irregular-shaped peg that stopped looking for its hole years ago. We are an unusual people—our history, language, cuisine, environment, traditions, ethnic makeup, and worldview are unique. Sure, we share some similarities with our neighbors, but there truly is no place like our home. There's also some intangible about being a home-grown product, and if you don't have it you'll stand out like a Pentecostal at Catholic Mass. This makes incursions by outsiders very noticeable. I may be a "born and raised Louisiana boy," but the day I visited those three church sites, I felt like an unwashed foreigner traipsing on sacred ground.

The first site I went to was Mt. Pleasant Baptist Church in southern Opelousas (pronounced "op-a-lew-sis). Mt. Pleasant was burned six days before the Lord prompted me to "just show up," so I was surprised by the number of local, state, and federal officials who were still investigating the remains. There were so many initialed polo shirts and windbreakers onsite, I couldn't even park to see the effects of the fire for myself. From the road, I could see the roof was gone. It just didn't exist anymore. The belfry had been badly damaged too, but that was all I could see. I was moved to tears at the roadside, but I left with a glimmer of hope—maybe the arsonist's attack had damaged the structures, but not destroyed them entirely. Maybe this wouldn't be as bad as it seemed for the congregation and the community as a whole.

As I drove toward Greater Union Baptist Church in east Opelousas, which was burned just two days before Mt. Pleasant, a coward's thought entered my mind: what if God simply wants me to draw attention to these traves-ties? Sure, I'm no social media star, but I know plenty of people with huge followings. Maybe one of them will repost my pictures. What if that's the difference he wants me to make? Maybe "showing up" really is all he wanted me to do. In my gut, I didn't believe that, but part of me wanted it to be true. The last thing these people need is some random white guy on their doorstep crying about racial injustice. How are they supposed to know if the tears are genuine? They need to hunker down and weather the storm, not take in some unfamiliar passerby who looks like one of the law enforcement officers investi-gating the fire—I half prayed/half whined to the Lord. I'll do more harm than good.

It took me a while to find Greater Union Baptist, because Google Maps kept bringing me to another church in town. When I finally arrived, there was no one there; so, I parked by the street and started walking to the main building. At first, much like Mt. Pleasant, I saw the roof had gone up in the fire, but the front of the building seemed relatively untouched. Hope stirred again. As I got close enough to see behind the exterior brick wall facing the road, I was shocked. I kept looking through the twin doors to the sanctuary. Both had been clear glass in metal frames. The frames were contorted and the glass was gone. Inside was ash. The pews, floors, alter, hymnals, everything was just ash. There was no saving this sanctuary. It was totally incinerated.

I fell apart. I am not a lover of church buildings; I could really care less what type of structure houses a faith community. Beautiful architecture is wasted on me too, because aesthetics means almost nothing to me. It was the history I mourned, not the bricks and mortar. One hundred and eleven years of baptisms, graduations, birthdays, sermons, salvations, marriages, funerals... one hundred and eleven years as the bedrock of the community. Reduced to nothing. Reverend Andrew Smith, the founding pastor, shepherded his flock at Greater Union Baptist for 55 years. As a member of the Charismatic Movement, that kind of stability was staggering to me. Now, the stone of remembrance for this community was gone.

Remember all those stone monuments God had the Israelites erect throughout the land of Canaan? They were focal points of their faith, placed strategically to remind the people God was for them. For these modern-day children of God, it was as if a Philistine hoard had removed their stone of remembrance, their monument to the faithfulness of God. It was a visceral loss. If it would have happened accidentally, it would have been heartbreaking. For it to have happened as an act of terror was sickening. How could someone do this? Why? How many more churches would these maniacs torch before their hate-filled rage was slated? In the face of senseless destruction, we find more questions than answers. I just kept staring through those broken doors into the charred remnant of what was once a sanctuary. Doors of a church should lead to family, compassion, truth, power, and above all love. These led to ash. The reality of what was left jarred me. I couldn't stop crying. What could anyone do in the face of such destructive hate?

If there was even a chance He would provide an opportunity for me to serve these people, His children going through hell, who was I not to show up?

— WES BROUSSARD

CHAPTER FIVE

Do Unto Others

How I treat a brother or sister from day to day, how I react to the sin-scarred wino on the street, how I respond to interruptions from people I dislike, how I deal with normal people in their normal confusion on a normal day, may be a better indication of my reverence for life than the anti-abortion sticker on the bumper of my car.

— BRENNAN MANNING

A THOUGHT CAME to mind as I drove away from Greater Union: ghost town. Unlike Mt. Pleasant, which was overrun with a wide variety of government agents,

Greater Union felt absolutely abandoned. I was there for nearly an hour and didn't see another soul. I'm sure people came when it first burned down, but that was eight days before I arrived. By that time, another arsonist's attack had taken place across town; so, Greater Union was left deserted. Understandably, the attention had moved on to the next site. Unfortunately, the people couldn't. While the world moved on, they were left to sift through the ashes, literally.

An eerie, hollow feeling followed me out of Opelousas. Obviously, it's disturbing to see such desolation, but the sense that this "middle child" of the three burnings was already left unattended was deflating. I understood it. What good would come from hanging out there in the afternoon on a random Wednesday? The insurance adjustments were probably done. The police had another, more recent site to investigate. The press had an even larger story to cover with a third attack in nine days; so, why would anyone be there? I get it. Still, I felt the twinge of institutionalized negligence. If these churches were located in a large city or were predominantly white, would they be a ghost town only a week after being torched?

I tried to imagine the scenario taking place at the mega-church where I had been a member and staffer for almost a decade, since I first gave my life to Christ. By the eighth day, we would have cleared the ruins away. Within a month, we would have started new construction with a fund-raising campaign designed to take back what the enemy stole from us. The proud, almost entirely middle-class white congregation would have raised money, provided labor, donated materials, and broke ground on a new and improved facility before the ink was dry on the first of many insurance checks. The more affluent members would have covered huge, anonymous needs with the stroke of a pen. In very little time at all, our facilities would have been grander than ever. What the hate-mongers would have intended for evil, God's people would have used for good. Was any of this true for the people of God in the quiet town of Opelousas? I didn't know, but something inside me said their road to resurgence would be much more difficult.

There is nothing wrong with being blessed, organized, well-funded, and capable of handling tragedy—that's wonderful. But if you'd raise money and sacrifice for your home church, which has only existed for a decade and was one of a handful you attended, why wouldn't you contend for the pillar of your brothers' community that had stood as the defining fabric of their culture since the early 1900's? Doesn't God say to bear one another's burdens? Doesn't He say love endures all things? Doesn't He say to fail to show love for your brother proves you don't love God? How do we justify not caring about the very people who our King bled and died to save? How do we call ourselves Christians when we really only care about our little corner of the Kingdom? Are we really in the Kingdom at all if we aren't connected to the other corners? I'm not saying we need to constantly be at each other's houses, but if someone burns down their churches, maybe we should show up. This is a family, after all. It warrants more than a crying emoji or arguing politics and doctrine on social media. What can I do? Where do I start?

This line of thinking was leading me down a dark path. Sure, the questions were sound, at least in the beginning, but the logic soon became cyclical and defeatist. Also, it pointed the finger at everyone else, so I didn't have to consider my own selfishness in dealing with the task at hand. I was ducking my fear and doubt by griping about the state of the church. A typical trap, but a successful one nonetheless. Useless arguments never lead to Kingdom results, but this one opened a particularly foul door. I felt like a black hole was pulling me into its crushing void. It was all I could do to keep my SUV pointed in the right direction.

CHAPTER SIX

Did He Really Say...

In a fight, your doubt is a target of (your) enemy's attack.

— TOBA BETH

WITH THESE FRUSTRATINGLY UNANSWERABLE questions careening off the walls of my mind, I drove to my last scheduled stop, the church which was burned first—St. Mary's Missionary Baptist in Port Barre, LA. Though the trip only took fifteen minutes, it seemed like hours. Emotionally, I was unraveling. The questions about unity and family were hounding me, as they had for most of my Christian life. I'd been a pastor several times, in multiple states, within multiple denominations. I'd preached countless long-winded sermons, counseled hundreds of distressed people, and fought the good fight for a little over eighteen years. Nevertheless, in all my experience I'd never faced racism, wreckage, or emptiness like this.

It is extremely rare for me to give the enemy of our soul much attention, because Jesus put him under our feet before we took our first steps. Still, in that moment I recognized his taunts of derision and despair. He was mocking me. For the sake of transparency and testimony, I'll share his lies with you now. Perhaps you've heard them, too:

How could a piece of white trash from a dirt road in a hole-in-the-wall like Prairieville expect to make any difference, when hundreds of thousands of pastors all over America can't get their congregations to tithe, stop gossiping, or actually love their neighbor? Are you really going to show up in your hubris and make a bad situation worse? This is like crashing the funeral of a stranger's beloved great-grandfather and knocking over the casket in the middle of "Amazing Grace." You are an idiot, a scared little boy who dreamed big dreams but couldn't even keep his own house together. This is arrogance. This is stupidity. Do the right thing and leave these wounded people to grieve. The last thing they need is a man who probably looks just like the monster who charred their church showing up with no idea what he's doing, fumbling over his good intentions, and insulting their pain. Why are you driving to this last church, when you know He is just going to leave you out to dry when you get there? How many times does He have to desert you in ministry before you realize your dreams are simply unachievable, especially for you? People don't want unity, family, or vulnerability... and most of all they don't want you. You are unlovable, unwanted, a disaster looking for a place to make landfall. Leave. If you claim to love these people, then turn around. Turn around in that driveway. You will turn around. You know you can't risk another beating at the hands of Christians. Look, there's a spot. No? Go ahead then. See what happens. You know He's going to do something and you know it will not end well. Following him never does.

The weight of foreboding was crushing me. God was going to do something—I knew it, and so did my enemy. The bastard threw everything at me. I almost turned around half a dozen times before I found the remains of St. Mary's, sitting on a little hill just off Highway 103. To my immediate relief and shame, no one was there.

Doesn't God say to bear one another's burdens? Doesn't He say love endures all things? Doesn't He say to fail to show love for your brother proves you don't love God? How do we justify not caring about the very people who our King bled and died to save? How do we call ourselves Christians when we really only care about our little corner of the Kingdom? Are we really in the Kingdom at all if we aren't connected to the other corners?

— WES BROUSSARD

CHAPTER SEVEN

Never Met a Stranger

It's good to remember that in crises, natural crises, human beings forget for awhile their ignorances, their biases, their prejudices. For a little while, neighbors help neighbors and strangers help strangers.

— *MAYA ANGELOU*

THERE WAS no glimmer of hope here, not that hope would have survived my experience at Greater Union anyway. The damage was unmistakable and irrevocable. The shock of seeing these houses of worship burned was anew each time, but there was a new level at St. Mary's:

burned Bibles strewn amongst the rubble. His precious word, torched by hate. Until very recently in the grand scope of human history, people didn't own Bibles. To this day, in some restricted countries, even ministers don't own a copy. The history of the printing and dissemination of the Bible is a beautiful tragedy, filled with courage and pain. People have been hunted, beaten, slandered, and murdered for even speaking the words of Scripture. These copies on the floor of St. Mary's would never be read again. How many hands had held these Bibles? How many children had studied the maps in the back of the sacred book during "big church"? How many times had the eternal and priceless words of God ministered to his children through these bound pages? Now, they were unredeemable. Even touching the books turned large portions into ash.

There was another door. Its frame was wrenched from the brick and tossed several feet from the remains of the building. Choosing to "darken the doorway" of a church has been the starting point for millions of people looking for truth, beauty, and goodness in this life. This doorway would never be used again. Yes, rebuilding was an option. No, this wasn't the end all, be all. It was, however, depressing and horrible. I was hanging around, taking pictures, waiting for God to do something for 45 minutes. Nothing was happening. A small work crew came and left. A few cars drove by on the sleepy state highway. I saw a poster someone had made and left on site, encouraging the believers with Acts 14:22: "... where they strengthened the believers. They encouraged them to continue in the faith, reminding them that we must suffer many hardships to enter the Kingdom of God." The white poster seemed out of place among the debris; so did I.

Seeing a Bible that was entirely charred, I used a plastic bag to put what was left on my passenger side floorboard. Maybe I'd order a display case and keep it at home. Reluctant to leave, I prayed God would send someone to connect with me. I went back through the articles I'd read, trying to find a possible connection point there, but found nothing. I felt like I'd done what God asked, but wasn't satisfied with the results. I waited a little longer, playing Words with Friends on my phone to pass the time. Then a truck pulled up. An older black gentleman rolled down his window, so I walked over to greet him. He was smiling and had kind, observant eyes. He asked me what "team" I was with, which puzzled me. He clarified, "Police, FBI, which team?" I stammered a response, "Oh, none of those... I guess I'm with... t-team Jesus." That was the right answer. His smile broadened and he introduced himself to me again, re-shaking my hand as a fellow believer. I felt hope stirring. We talked for 30 minutes about the fires, insurance, the police investigation, and the community's response. I learned his name, Mr. Joe Lea (pronounced Lee), and his impressive life story. Mr. Joe joined the Air Force in his youth. After 20 years in the military, he retired and began his second career as an electrician with a local contractor. Decades later, he retired from his craft and became a sugar cane farmer, which was his current profession. Also, he had been a deacon at St. Mary's for longer than I'd been alive. Members of his family and community had been attending this church for decades. In his 82 years, he'd lived quite a life.

There was nothing hesitant or distant in Mr. Joe's manner. He treated me like a friend. The differences in our ages, races, and life experiences didn't seem to matter to this man, despite the divisive hardship he was immersed in at the moment. To put it simply, he was loving. He was the loving brother I needed to find. I was hoping to show God's love to the people of his community, but it was Mr. Joe who rescued me. The grace his acceptance released over me was cathartic and redemptive.

CHAPTER EIGHT

Poignant Love

There is something wonderful in seeing a wrong-headed majority assailed by truth.

— JOHN KENNETH GALBRAITH

As Mr. Joe talked about the Wednesday night prayer service being held a couple of hours later, only a few miles away, I heard that still small voice again. As I began to ratchet up my courage to ask about attending the prayer service as his guest, the liar's voice spoke up too. I won't go into detail, because I've given the enemy enough attention already, but it was more of the same.

I felt myself chickening out.

I led the conversation toward fundraising, awareness, and helping to connect St. Mary's to her sister churches in the Greater Baton Rouge Area for additional support. Mr. Joe was content to allow the conversation to die this death. The wisdom of his life experiences probably told him I was a well-intentioned young man, who at least cared enough to show up, but who he'd probably never see again. We were past the point of being conversationally awkward, so I gave him my card and promised to stay connected to the rebuilding process.

As I walked to my SUV, I knew I'd failed. I couldn't know the far-reaching effects of my failure, but I knew I'd blown it. I slumped into the driver's seat and slowly closed the door. I watched as Mr. Joe started a little chore he'd mentioned, but assured me he didn't need my help to accomplish. The atmosphere was stagnant with my cowardice. After what seemed like a stint in purgatory, I started the engine and headed back south on Highway 103. I was crying, cussing, depressed, and angry. Why couldn't God understand that inviting myself to their family-style prayer service only nine days after their church was burned to the ground by a white supremacist was unthinkable!? Why wouldn't this conviction subside and let me be? The lies were attempting to pry their way into my conversation with God, but it was the truth that was assailing me at that point. I'd determined I knew better than God, so I disobeyed him. I was no better than Adam in the Garden.

The gentle voice of love asked me poignantly, Do you know what good could come from this? Can you see the end from the beginning? Where were you when I lovingly formed my children in their mothers' wombs? What if I truly sent you here—what good will you withhold from my kids if you tell me No? There's a place. Turn around. You can still catch my son, Mr. Joe. He's still there, where I positioned him for you.

This time, I turned around.

God was going to do something—I knew it, and so did my enemy.

— WES BROUSSARD

CHAPTER NINE

Polite Awkwardness

When people are perfectly polite, it usually means they don't really care. A little awkwardness is more sincere.

— KEN FOLLETT

AFTER A TIRE-SCREECHING drive back to St. Mary's, I found Mr. Joe—still there, just as my Father had promised. My reappearance brought a quizzical look to his face, but I didn't waste any time with preamble. "Mr. Joe," I asked, "that prayer service tonight, would it be okay if I attended?" He hesitated for the slightest beat, no more than a second, before he responded, "Yes. Yes, you can. We'd love to have you." His tone was slightly cautious, but welcoming. As he smiled at me, my fears and anxiety melted. Not because my task was complete—I knew this was only the entrance exam—but because I'd crossed the threshold. From here, there was no going back. Thank God.

We exchanged logistical information and parted ways until the service. I had a couple of hours to waste; so, not being familiar with the town, I drove around to get my bearings. As I drove, I noticed Opelousas is like a lot of small Louisiana towns: historic, set in its ways, and full of interesting extremes. For example, there's a racetrack and casino within ten miles of at least 20 churches. The airport for St. Landry's Parish is just north of town, but the town itself only boasts 16,000 residents. Back in 2004, the city annexed territory, expecting the population to balloon above 25,000; but the 2008 Recession hit the town and its people hard. They lost almost 30% of their residents in less than a year. Since we all know prices haven't gone down in the last decade, the people are trying to do more with less, and you can feel the struggle as you drive through the city.

There's the typical racial divide, too. Not knowing the "black side of town" from the "white side of town" (yes, that still exists in a lot of places down here), I just looked for the closest gas station. I could feel the mistrust and even disdain as I got gas, drove through residential areas in my ten-year-old Lincoln, and pulled up at Chicken King. Most of the black people I encountered did very little to hide their misgivings. "You are an interloper, and it's best you realize that upfront," was the sentiment relayed by some of the more unpleasant looks. Others simply looked surprised and curious.

The experience brought to mind being the only white kid on basketball teams growing up, and the looks my teammates would give me as we dressed out for our games. Having never seen a white person with their shirt off up close, they'd steal glances out of the corners of their eyes. Eventually, the guys would give up decorum and outright stare at me like an exhibit at the zoo. Once we got closer, they'd ask questions about my body hair, if the world looked different out of blue eyes, how often I got my hair cut, why I didn't look ripped even though I was strong, etc. Some of the older guys would roll their eyes and cluck their tongues, but I thought it was important to have those conversations. It disarmed our differences to a degree. We'd use the same sweat rags and drink from the same water bottles, which raised eyebrows. But we would just laugh and say, "We're brothers. That's what we do."

On my drive through town, I wished I could have played ball in Opelousas as a kid. Maybe then they wouldn't see an intruder or an oddity, but a brother, especially a brother in Christ. As I drove, I thought back to the first black men I'd known, and how their impact would define "black" for me, even as a very young boy.

SECTION TWO: DEFINING MOMENTS

.....This time, I turned around.

— WES BROUSSARD

CHAPTER TEN

Examples A & B

The world is changed by your example, not by your opinion.

— PAULO COELHO

MR. KEITH CANN and Mr. Hank Williams helped define my vocabulary and my opinions about black men at a very early age. Mr. Keith had aspirations of becoming a genuine cowboy, so he trained with my father, Cecil Broussard. Back in the 1970's, my dad won some of the biggest rodeos in the world on his way to a very successful, albeit physically grueling, career. He also trained multiple world champion horses and cowboys throughout his life-time, so Mr. Keith wasn't alone in seeking my dad's tutelage.

Rodeo culture at the time was brutal—men carried concealed pistols at all times; losers would steal prize money at gunpoint; adultery was more common than fidelity; officials would cheat to give certain contestants the upper hand; cowboys would sneak livestock across quarantine lines in U-Haul trailers; drug-induced, all night drives were standard; etc. This was no place for a "nice guy." Still, that's exactly what Mr. Keith was. He was tough and took more than his fair share of guff, so my dad was happy to have him around; but he didn't have that cruel streak in him. He never let the rampant toxic masculinity convince him he needed to prove his "manliness."

Just like my dad before me, I grew up in my father's world, so there were only a few men like Mr. Keith in my life. He was the first black man I knew, and one of the only kind-hearted men with enough toughness to survive rodeo culture. Through his example, I learned the intrinsic value of both manhood and the African-Amer-ican community. If someone didn't like Mr. Keith, some-thing was wrong with them, not him. I am well aware he was just another imperfect human, but he always treated me well, even though most of the others didn't. They saw a boy as someone to toughen up in hopes of helping him become a "real man" one day. For some reason, they couldn't see how badly that treatment had failed in making them into men; so, they kept feeding the broken cycle. Even as a kid, I knew that was stupid. Toughness is necessary in life; but without kindness, it's not a life worth living. There has to be gentleness in the eyes of a man to make him a man. Mr. Keith taught me that.

Mr. Hank Williams, not the singer, was a Sheriff's Deputy in my hometown. Like Mr. Keith, Mr. Hank was no pushover. He wore a gun, spoke plainly, and treated everyone equally. I first met him when I was very young, then saw him almost every Friday night for several years at my favorite childhood haunt: Colonial Skateland. For the most part, the "Skating Ring" was a decent place to play video games, skate, dance, and meet your first girl-friend. On its worst nights, however, a kid brought a gun, older kids beat up tweens, and young teenagers lost their virginity in dimly lit corners. When Mr. Hank was nearby, the entire atmosphere changed. Even the hell-raisers didn't challenge Mr. Hank. He was funny, patient, and thoughtful. He loved to ask kids, "Hey, where's my $5? You know! The $5 you owe me—where is it?" While some older teens didn't get it, us younger kids got a kick out of an adult asking us where we put his money... especially a tall black man with a gun! He had a way of cutting through your preconceptions, so you had to deal with him as an individual. Not as a cop or a black man, but as Mr. Hank.

I have a few good stories about Mr. Hank, but my most vivid memory still grates on my spirit. I was getting to know this new kid, which was great, because I didn't have a ton of friends. We were both good skaters, so we were doing what boys do: racing. As we made our laps, he got close to where Mr. Hank was standing on the other side of a four-foot-high wall. Out of nowhere, the kid called Mr. Hank a nigger, then bolted off before a very fast black hand could grab him. It unnerved me. I'd heard the term hundreds of times, but could never imagine someone throwing it at Mr. Hank. To use it as a weapon against an honorable man was unforgivable. For Mr. Hank, sadly, it wasn't uncommon. I could tell, because after his swipe missed the young man's head, he collected himself, his stern face softened into shameful resignation, and he walked away. The kid skated off laughing and smiling at me, as if he'd just proven how tough and masculine he was by insulting a good man and getting away with it. Sure, Mr. Hank could've hemmed him up and thrown him in the back of a squad car, but in the end nothing would happen to the kid. God forbid the little jerk be a politician's boy or a fellow officer's son, then Mr. Hank would have been in the middle of a serious storm. As a black man in south Louisiana in the early 1990s, the smart move was to let the punk go, trusting he'd reap what he sowed eventually.

To this day, I find racism difficult to forgive. God is working with me to see all sin as equal, to realize I am no better than the racist I want to pass judgment on, because we are all buried in our sin without the sweet blood of Jesus. I've had classmates, co-workers, family members, and ministry partners act like bigots around black folks just to push my buttons. As recently as this month, I had a client spout some old-school racist drivel trying to provoke me, because he knows where I stand. For me, when I hear that garbage, my fight or flight reflex goes off. I feel some tiny part of the weight of the oppression of millions of people bearing down on my soul, and I fight back. Usually. To be honest, sometimes I just walk away. Some people aren't worth getting into "fight mode" with, but I always feel guilty. It's like I failed Mr. Keith or Mr. Hank, or any one of a dozen close friends by not fighting back. I haven't figured this out, but there has to be more I can do. For that 12-year-old boy to have such power in the form of a single word over a strong man like Mr. Hank is unbearable. That was 25 years ago, but I can still see his face. He knew there was nothing he could do. Even as a grown man and an experienced cop, he was helpless. As I thought about Mr. Hank, Mr. Keith, my basketball brothers, and my odd role in this enormous tapestry, another chilling incident came to mind.

CHAPTER ELEVEN

N.O.N.N.R.

It did not happen all at once. We did not wake up one morning to hear it pouring out of the radio at full strength. It started with a sneering comment, the casual use of the term "cockroach," the almost humorous suggestion that Tutsis should be airmailed back to Ethiopia. Stripping the humanity from an entire group of people takes time. It is an attitude that requires cultivation, a series of small steps, daily tending.

— PAUL RUSESABAGINA,
*DISCUSSING RWANDA BEFORE THE
1994 GENOCIDE*

IN 2006 I was a newly married college dropout looking for a career that wouldn't interfere with my eventual role as a full-time minister. While much of that last sentence is now humorous to me, at the time I was very committed to that line of logic. After striking out a few times, a high school friend offered to help me start a career as a firefighter in a nearby town. The pay was awful, but the steady income and time off would leave room for ministry as an additional income stream. Plus, firefighters save people! They are servants of the community and even heroes at times. What red-blooded American man wouldn't like the sound of that?

My friend came up with a plan: I would volunteer at the firehouse to earn the trust and respect of the established captains and my future fellow firemen before the upcoming open-hire period began. I had just over a month to prove myself, get someone to take a chance on me, and earn my place on the team. As a lover of team sports and the familiar dynamics found in that world, I took the challenge in stride. I would volunteer every day that I could, after working my temporary but full-time job as an equipment operator and fuel truck driver. It would be exhausting but rewarding, I concluded.

Immediately upon arriving for my first day of volunteering, my friend introduced me to his shift captain. The captain was very professional, with just enough warmth to show he was a decent human as well. Although he was a small black man in an otherwise burly white world, he commanded the respect and loyalty of his men without raising his voice or abusing his power. He had earned their trust through decency and excellence. He had wanted to be a fireman all his life. As I met others in authority, I knew this was the man I wanted supporting my efforts. With his backing, I'd have a legitimate shot at not only becoming a fireman, but at learning the craft from someone who could mentor me for years to come.

During my second day with my friend's group, we received a call to assist EMTs at a car accident ten minutes away. It was my first time inside the fire truck with the sirens blaring and the traffic yielding. To say it was a rush would be an understatement. As we arrived on the scene, we saw a black mother lodged in the front seat of a GMC Jimmy. I knew she was a mother, because her children were standing, unharmed, on the side of the road beside the contorted SUV. They were shaken up, and obviously concerned for their mother. I had absolutely no idea what to do, so I retrieved blankets from the truck for the kids and spoke kindly to them as the real firemen set up the jaws of life. Up until that exact moment, I thought the jaws of life were just a euphemism. I had no idea they resembled actual jaws, used for tearing apart metal to reach otherwise unreachable victims.

Between the traffic on Highway 44, the power source for the jaws of life, and the metal being mangled, the sound was deafening. I continued to sooth the children, but I was otherwise a waste of a jumpsuit. Not that I wanted to be involved necessarily—I was happy to sit back and observe as the utterly green rookie of the bunch. The aforementioned captain had other ideas. I kept catching his glance towards me as I knelt down and took care of the five children who'd been scrunched into the GMC. I wasn't being nice to black kids to court his favor, but I could see my response to the situation was drawing his curiosity. As the real heroes finished carving the driver's side door like a Thanksgiving turkey, my new captain gave me clear, loud instructions to take the woman out of the SUV. The others looked up and backed away so I could follow his command. With no idea how to correctly accomplish the task at hand, I hesitated, looking at him for guidance. He gave the order once again with a look that said, "I told you to do something—what are you waiting for?!" With that, I dove in head first.

But it was no easy task. The driver and I probably weighed the same amount. She was still partially trapped between the seat and the steering wheel, and limp from emotional hysteria, which was completely understandable. I reached in behind her lower back and under her knees and pulled her straight to me as I crouched down on the uneven ground outside her door. She actually slid out fairly easily, to my intense surprise and relief. Once she was clear of the driver's seat, the captain ordered the other men to assist me. They patted me on the back and rewarded me with light praise as I obeyed their leader. The captain, for his part, stared at me for a few seconds. I will probably never know what he was thinking, but from that day on he fought to get me on his team.

I tried to align my volunteer schedule with this captain's shifts, but that wasn't always possible. At times, I'd end up with other captains and their crews who didn't know me at all. I learned very little during these shifts, but I was dedicated to making a name for myself, so I was dutiful and quiet. The crews were never cruel, but there was the typical hazing and grunt work one would expect. Once the work was done, we'd spend a lot of time in a small office listening to the dispatch radio. Honestly, it was extremely boring. Even most of the emergency calls were mundane. Then it happened.

One of the other shifts' leaders who worked for one of the other captains was a loud mouth, overweight bully looking for someone to push down. He was gross to me. I'd known men like that all my life and knew they were best avoided when in power. He would make dumb jokes and stare at you to make sure you laughed. He was a real power trip falling all over himself to make sure everyone knew he was a tough, no-nonsense authority figure. He was an imbecile.

I was almost never in the same room as him, but one day I ended up sitting with him and a few others for hours as we listened to the incoming calls. While there were numerous emergencies, most were outside of our territory. We waited for long minutes between calls, suffering the humor of our fearless leader. Suddenly, a woman's voice called out a life and death scenario a mile and a half from the firehouse:

"Reports of a shooting at the corner of HWY 30 and Veterans." Even though shootings are primarily a police matter, our firehouse served as the local EMT facility. We could have an ambulance there in under five minutes, I thought, but said nothing as I suppressed my adrenaline.

"First suspect is a black male, mid 20's, nearly six feet tall." The tension in the room was just short of tangible. "The second suspect is a black male, mid 20's, six feet tall..." The volume on the radio was turned down to a whisper. Four heads jerked towards the radio to see the shift leader with his hand on the dial.

"N.O.N.N.R.," was his arrogant, dismissive explanation. Taking a quick survey of the room, I saw one man laugh jeeringly, one younger man stare blankly, and two men's eyes drop to the floor. Finding no resolution to my obvious question, I looked back at the neanderthal controlling the radio.

"What does N.O.N.N.R. mean?" I impatiently asked as crucial seconds slipped away. He replied, "Nigger On Nigger No Rush."

I was hoping to show God's love to the people of his community, but it was Mr. Joe who rescued me.

— WES BROUSSARD

CHAPTER TWELVE

Objects in the Mirror...

The past is never where you think you left it.

— KATHERINE ANNE PORTER

I'VE HAD HALF a dozen accountability partners over the two decades of my Christianity. Two of those fine gentlemen were black: Carl and Reggie. Carl and I were roommates for a couple of years, until I got married back in 2006. It's safe to say Carl was my closest friend during that time. He was a deep and convicted person, but also mercurial. Reggie and I met at church and became dear friends through years of playing ball, suffering through tragedies, and raising families together. These are two of my all-time favorite people.

Carl and I had great conversations—some of the best of my life. We would grab a bite to eat or sit around the apartment for hours discussing the deepest, most awe-inspiring aspects of life. During one of these marathon talks we landed on the topic of racism. I talked about growing up five minutes from the KKK leader of my hometown, going to school with secretive junior Klan members, and how friends of mine had been told by realtors they couldn't live in certain neighborhoods if they didn't "fly sheets" (i.e. support the KKK). While these stories were quite shocking to my white friends and my black friends from other parts of the country, Carl just smiled his sad-eyed smile... then he stopped smiling. Slowly, cautiously, Carl told me about what he experienced as a child. Carl's mother was barely a teenager when she became pregnant with him, and his father was locked up in Angola for most of Carl's life (Angola is the infamous state prison where The Green Mile was filmed). His mother was his hero, because she managed to survive the ordeal and even provide Carl the opportunity to attend a four-year college, which he did. The financial hardships were unspeakable, but they made a way where there was virtually no way. He and his mother are living, breathing miracles in my eyes.

Livingston, Carl's hometown, is only 30 minutes from the state capital of Baton Rouge, but it's a different world. Honestly, it's a lot like Opelousas: small, racially divided, and in some ways very poor. In these small pockets, hate doesn't just exist—it thrives. Having grown up in a similar small town not far away, I knew this all too well; but the pain and distance in Carl's face as he opened up about his experiences were unsettling me. Carl was a rock, but he had to numb himself to address these memories. I'd never seen him like that. While there were multiple experiences with racism, the most striking one occurred when Carl had the audacity to have a relationship with a white girl in his school. Classmates lashed out at him, starting fights on a daily basis. Eventually, his life was threatened to the point he didn't leave his home for several months. His mother conquered unbelievable obstacles to put her son through college, something many well-to-do white folks can't even do, but she was powerless against a private citizen wanting to terrorize her family.

While Reggie's upbringing was quite different, parts of his story were strikingly similar. He grew up in Jefferson Parish, near New Orleans. His family was and is intact. They were not wealthy by any means, but they weren't poor either. Reggie, like Carl, excelled in sports. Reggie was also the life of any room he walked into—his larger than life smile, laugh, and hugs still light up faces everywhere he goes. Once, after not seeing him for about a year, I bumped into him at church. He football tackled me into a wall during the tithe and offering! Like I said, he's one of my favorites.

During one of our longer sit-downs, Reggie shared a story similar to Carl's. His face didn't go unhinged in the way Carl's did, but his eyes dimmed and his tone flattened, which is unheard of for this energy-jolt of a man. He described a morning fishing trip with his dad, which was a pleasant memory. As they arrived home, young Reggie and his father discovered a KKK cross driven into their front yard. The white supremacists used the symbol of perfect love to infer their infernal message of damnable hate. What sick, depraved minds. To make matters worse, Reggie knew the kid who admitted to putting the cross in his yard. Unfortunately, the boy was also a sheriff's deputy's son.

Reggie's family handled the situation with brilliance and dogged toughness, so much so that Reggie didn't carry any residual hate with him into adulthood. I don't really understand, because I struggle with it as a grown man just hearing the story years later. I asked Reggie to revisit the criminal incident with his family as I was writing this book. In their wisdom, his father and mother decided to pursue the criminals, but not the charges. I don't want to put words in their mouths, so I'll quote them here. His dad's sentiment was short and strong: "Not all black people are as stupid and ignorant as y'all are." Well, that's certainly true. His mom's thoughts were a little more comprehensive:

I was thinking, "Could anyone be so naïve?" There were other black families that lived in the subdivision. I asked the officer, "Just remind me we're in the 20th century?" Also asked him about getting fingerprints to which he replied, "No." It was wood and paint... What's ironic is that they thought we wouldn't do anything. This was not the 1800s. We, with due diligence from a friend who was a lawyer, found out who it was. His father was a police officer. The old expression "The apple doesn't fall far from the tree" came to mind.

Reggie's parents decided to require the young man to show up at their home and apologize to them face to face, instead of pressing serious charges. His mom recounts the experience:

They came all humble and apologetic, but I said, "Are you aware you could have a federal criminal record for a racially motivated hate crime?"

We didn't press charges, but made it clear that those days were over. Does racism still exist? Yes, but it has a whole different face. May we pray that we have peace, faith, hope and love in our hearts!

Reggie's family was much braver and more forgiving than I would have been. If my fifteen-year-old ever comes home to a cross in our yard, I hope I handle the situation with similar dignity.

Unfortunately for Reggie, the story didn't end there. A few days later, a group of white kids at school singled him out and started mocking him for being the target of a hate crime. To this day, the helplessness in his voice and eyes as he recounts this part of the story breaks me. He couldn't fight without getting jumped, which is a guaranteed beating. He couldn't slink away without looking scared and pathetic. All he could do was stand there and take it. Following the example of his parents, he counted the costs, made his decision, and stood in all the strength he could muster for the moment.

Two close friends, both survivors of oppression and

terror. Two families, wondering if that would be the extent of the damage. Parents who don't know what to tell their children. Do you tell your sons to play life small, which proves the threat of violence works and empowers the racists to continue using that strategy? Do you tell your sons to take up as much space in life as they can, and play Russian roulette with your family's safety? Maybe they were empty threats, or maybe the despicable crimes were opening salvos before the real fight began. What would you tell your sons? To make matters worse, there were no consequences for the hate-mongers. There was no hope of justice. Some people wonder why black Americans seem so angry or why the Black Lives Matter movement seems so aggressive. These are just a few of the stories I know. How many more Carls, Reggies, and Mr. Hanks are out there? As the empathy swelled my heart, a more recent memory came back to me.

To this day, I find racism difficult to forgive.

— WES BROUSSARD

CHAPTER THIRTEEN

Memphis Mission

Too much blood has been shed for anything less than love.

— WES BROUSSARD

SIX MONTHS before my encounter with the Lord on I-10, I felt the him leading me to attend a concert for Lecrae Moore and Andy Mineo in Memphis, Tennessee. Much like my journey to central Louisiana, this was an adventurous mission. It was adventurous because those are two incredible artists (Lecrae is possibly my all-time favorite in any genre). It was a mission because he was sending me with a message. A message I was terrified to deliver to a man I didn't know from Adam, but who had been deeply wounded by Christians.

Several years ago, you couldn't turn on the news without hearing about police brutality against black people. Some of the cases were fraudulent and ridiculous. Some were equally ridiculous, but undeniably true. In response, the Black Lives Matter movement started. It was an imperfect group of people trying to make a point out of two very valid but polarizing emotions: anger and fear. Blue Lives Matter came next, as a response to the BLM movement. America was freshly divided, and the division was all anyone would talk about. As artists often do, Lecrae and Andy Mineo attempted to tackle these issues with transparency and as much objectivity as possible. For their efforts to mend our splintered society, they were met with disgust and ignorance. Over the next few years, there was intense betrayal and abandonment from long-time supporters, trusted voices, and a significant portion of their fan base. As I am more connected with Lecrae musically, I felt more connected to his burden. As he vulnerably breached the topics of hate letters and threats, I couldn't believe what people were saying. What Christians were saying to another believer was toxic. All of a sudden, the old racial lines their artistry and authenticity had soothed were as visible and jarring as police lights in your rear view mirror.

Despite the backlash, many Christian artists who spoke up really believed their brothers and sisters in the faith would see their point of view and attempt to support them. Bye and large, they were dead wrong. As far as social media commentary goes, I saw one man who claimed God killed Lecrae's son because of his beliefs (he wrote it just that bluntly). Now as awful as that is to say, let alone believe, it's equally stupid. Lecrae has never lost any of his children. I can't imagine uttering something so foul; but to say it to someone who you believe has lost their son... there are no words.

Why do racially driven topics dredge up this level or animosity, especially among Christians? Shouldn't we always seek to support one another, even in disagreement (Ephesians 4)? Shouldn't love and honor always be the objective (1st John 1, 1st Corinthians 13)? How does the love of God take a backseat to the irrational judgment of man whenever we have to deal with these issues (Isaiah 55)? It's mystifying and disheartening.

I wish I could say I've never experienced those deep wounds myself, but my Christian journey has been fraught with other believers intentionally and sometimes systematically seeking to subvert my influence and reputa-tion. As a pastor who has always pushed for deep relation-ships amongst leadership, purposeful discipleship of parishioners, and commitment to social justice issues; I've definitely endured my fair share of bitter criticism and backstabbing. In those seasons, the feeling of helplessness makes the bile in your stomach seem weighted and diseased. I wish I could say my experiences were an anomaly, to steal a term from Mr. Moore, but they are not. Unfortunately, I see more and more of this abusive and negligent behavior every year.

I could relate to what Lecrae was going through, and I wanted him to know there were many of us who saw his valiant efforts and would support him no matter what. I wanted him to know he wasn't alone. So, with the leading of Holy Spirit, I bought a backstage pass for the closest concert. As I arrived at the venue several hours early, I saw that I would stick out like a sore thumb—a large, 30-something white man in "dad jeans" amongst a room full of trendy men and women wearing skinny jeans and graphic tees. As I stood in line for over an hour to have a brief photo opportunity with the two artists, my nerves started getting the better of me. I knew what God wanted me to say and how I wanted to say it, but how in the world would a man who had already paid such a high price value encouragement from a man who hadn't? Would Lecrae hear my heart, what I believe God sent me to say, or would the distance between our worlds make the void unbridgeable?

As Lecrae and Andy entered the room for the brief

introduction and photo session, those of us who had paid hundreds of dollars for this opportunity erupted into cheers. I had listened to every song Lecrae had ever released for thirteen years, most of them hundreds of times. In many ways, his lyrical journey mirrored my own walk with Christ. We both got radically saved, then became very intentional regarding mentorship, then found a wide range acceptance from unexpected audiences, then discovered that those audiences only accept you as long as you do what's acceptable to them. Lastly, we found that Jesus wasn't an American Christian—he is God. He is above and other and good. Because He is good and His love is untamable, He can be trusted with our most fragile places. The behavior of the children of God does not perfectly reflect His nature, so even if God's people fail you, He never will. I don't know if Lecrae would paraphrase his catalog of music the way I just did, but that's what I experienced as I journeyed with him from album to album. To meet him and thank him was easy and gratifying. Completing my mission, however, made me feel intensely aware of my skin color, age, weight, emotions, and failures.

As my turn to meet and greet started, I shook Andy's hand first and thanked him for the vulnerability in his music, but I quickly moved on to Lecrae. Sensing I was nervous, Andy kindly pulled me back toward him and asked me for my name and if I wanted a picture. I introduced myself and declined the photo. Though he had already reached out to make me comfortable, he let it go. Seeing this odd interchange just a few feet away seemed to lift Lecrae's eyebrows just a bit. I don't think he knew what to expect, but I got the feeling a small part of him guessed it wouldn't be good. Part of me wanted to play it cool—these were artists after all—but as I looked him in the eye and shook his hand, my voice broke and my eyes watered.

"Mr. Moore, because of stances you've taken, a lot of people who look just like me have turned their backs on you and even attacked you. They were wrong to do that. I'm so sorry they did."

That was all I could muster. I had a couple of other sentences I meant to add, but the moment was too intense for me. As a couple of fat tears rolled down my cheeks, Lecrae rocked back a little bit, his eyes widening in a look of deep surprise. For a brief moment, I had no idea what was coming. Then he pulled me in and hugged me hard. I don't remember what he said, unfortunately (it was something like a thank you), but I did get to add one more sentiment before I left: "Too much blood has been shed for anything less than love." As soon as I said that, he pulled back to look me in the eyes.

He quietly said, "Wow," then hugged me again. The

entire exchange took no more than 20 seconds. As I walked away from one of my heroes, I knew I'd completed my mission. I hoped it was what Lecrae needed at that moment. Knowing God, even though I felt like I fumbled it, I'm sure it was.

INNOCENCE

No innocence?
No coincidence!
That's just common sense
that's not common since
the system became a bottom line
Verdicts rendered without reason or rhyme
Policies turn on a dime
Justice that's never blind

Culture's shattered through and through
Lives don't matter, not Black, not blue
We NEED a reboot, need a mutiny
Not a tribute to disunity

To make America great again
We must confront our greatest sin
Nothing matters in our eyes
Until it disrupts our comfortable lives

— WES BROUSSARD

Why do racially driven topics dredge up animosity, especially among Christians? Shouldn't we always seek to support one another, even in disagreement?

— WES BROUSSARD

CHAPTER FOURTEEN

Comfort Food

Some of the strongest believers I know wear orange
on Sunday.

— WES BROUSSARD

BACK IN OPELOUSAS, I found something comforting as I
waited for the mid-week prayer service to start: good fried
chicken, courtesy of Chicken King. The taste and smell
brought me back to my grandmother's dining room, my
mother's kitchen, and a Popingo's gas station just outside
of Hunt's Correctional Facility in St. Gabriel, Louisiana.
In all honesty, I'd probably eaten Popingo's chicken more
than anybody else's (if you're not from the South, that

would be like eating gas station sushi more than your mom's spaghetti). Still, those two chicken breasts with fries and a Coke Icee were the launching point for a lot of fond memories. I would indulge in that routine treat almost every Thursday before prison ministry, or on Sundays after jail ministry, for five years. It was my go-to meal to commemorate the highlight of my week and prepare me for whatever fresh hell we had to tackle once we entered the razor wire kingdom.

I never anticipated getting involved with inmate ministry, but the call was unmistakable. If memory serves, it was 2010 when I volunteered to accompany my pastor to a prison revival. The entire experience was wrought with miscommunications and bad timing. Honestly, because of all the mishaps I was looking forward to leaving. On the way out the Sally ports, however, I was blessed to hear the testimony of Derek Lindsey. He spoke with such passion and clarity about the fourteen years he'd spent, on a strictly volunteer basis, working with the men within one of the most corrupt penal systems on the planet (Louisiana imprisons more people per capita for longer sentences than any country on Earth). Despite the bureaucratic red tape and unscrupulous dealings of politicians and correctional officers, Derek wholeheartedly believed in his mission as part of True Freedom inmate ministries. His intensity was contagious and I was hooked.

As I became part of the team, I discovered the source of Derek's passion: the founders of True Freedom, Ross English and Marvin Collins, had produced an unmistakably powerful tool for reconciling God's kids back to him. There were so many aspects I loved about their approach, but my favorite was probably that anything other than helping the men to develop a relationship with Holy Spirit was viewed as illegal contraband. To bring up denominations, religiosity, politics, racism, or any other lesser reality in the chapel would be treated like smuggling a gun or a pound of heroin into the warden's office. It was so refreshing to be part of a ministry that didn't idolize one man or one doctrine over another. We were simply there to walk hand in hand with these men as we all sought to know Jesus, the power of his resurrection, and the fellowship of his suffering (Philippians 3:10). It was the Gospel stripped down to its essential parts, and I loved it. It was certainly a challenge, but to this day some of the strongest believers I know wear orange on Sundays.

I have many fond memories of prison ministry, most of which are too personal to share. Of course, I had some sour experiences as well. Each of the facilities I worked in had their own vicious corrections officer. Both were ruthlessly cruel and suspicious, and not just toward the inmates (e.g. drug-sniffing dogs, pat-downs, invasive searches, and verbal harassment were not uncommon). Part of prison ministry is navigating the regimented day-to-day life of the inmates and guards, but some officers take it to an entirely different level simply for the power trip. It's jarring to be speaking to someone about the value they have in the eyes of their all-perfect, all-knowing, all-powerful Father God one minute, then to have some junior varsity reject with a Napoleon complex start screaming and spitting in their face over the most trivial or imagined offense the next. There were 2,200 men at Hunt's. The average sentence was over 20 years. Despair was part of the package—added humiliation for the sake of a small man's ego was beyond unnecessary. As disruptive as it was for us as volunteers, it was completely dehumanizing for the inmates.

I know, I know: if you can't do the time, don't do the crime. There is validity to that truism, but there's also such a thing as treating people like humans, even at their lowest point. We've all been hit by low points in life. If we are honest, most of the time we didn't even realize how far off the path we truly were until it was too late. With hindsight, it's easy to see where we went wrong, but in the moment it's very easy to make a bad situation much worse. I guess I'm trying to say these men's failures were complicated, just like every mess you or I've ever gotten ourselves into. As believers, we know the truth will set us free, but there are times when we are lost and have no idea what to do next.

Truth is always simple, but what do you say to people who've never heard the truth or read the Bible or known any genuine believers? Most of the men I mentored never met their fathers, were harshly abused throughout their childhoods, and the only Christians they ever knew were little old ladies with funny hats who spoke in the Elizabethan English of the King James Bible when they were angry. Sure, there were guys who found religion in prison, but their infatuation with Jailhouse Jesus rarely lasted past their release date. Some had families that went to church, but their faith never seemed to survive the car ride home from Sunday service. To know a genuine believer or hear unmolested truth in a practically applicable manner was a rarity. To encounter the love and holiness of God Almighty was nearly unheard of altogether. Maybe that's hard for some of you to believe, but I promise you it's true for more and more Americans each year.

This is the case in most of the US, because in the 21st century American church we cater to consumers when we should be making world-changers. I won't dive into that topic here, but Francis Chan's Letters to the Church is a bold treatise laid before the Church to focus on God, the body, and a languishing world rather than keep up with the technical aspects and marketing gimmicks of the church next door. It's a stunning read by a man who started a thriving mega church from his living room, then left it all at the height of his popularity to pursue God as he truly is. Nevertheless, Chan's books are not part of the prison library. Many of the men can't read anyway, and the prisons have little to no foundation on which to start building—especially in prisons that don't have amazing groups like True Freedom. Being in prison is like being in a third world country or a small diminishing town: whoever is in power lords it over those who aren't, creating a distinct sense of hopelessness and helplessness which is very difficult to overcome.

SECTION THREE: FAMILIES LOST AND FOUND

Calling people by their role in ministry is actually a reduction of their value. God always calls people by name, because a parent doesn't address their child by their title. Our value as God's kids is much higher than our value as His servants.

— WES BROUSSARD

CHAPTER FIFTEEN

Out of Place

I never felt comfortable with myself, because I was never part of the majority. I always felt awkward and shy and on the outside of the momentum of my friends' lives.

— STEVEN SPIELBERG

I FINISHED my chicken and thanked the delightful employees of Chicken King, then headed around the corner to the seemingly vacant building where St. Mary's Missionary Baptist Church started meeting after the fire. Per the norm, I was very early. As I waited, a strong peace came over me. The hard part was done. Now, all I had to do was be attentive and kind throughout the service. That was easy enough. Afterwards, who knows? Hopefully some kind of relationships would develop, but if nothing else I had been obedient.

As I sat in my SUV wrapping up calls and emails from work, several young people started hanging around the other store front buildings in the half-empty strip mall. Every person was curious of my presence. Most of them were kids who stared wide-eyed at me as they very slowly walked past. I just smiled and waved the customary one-motion hand gesture of men in the South. For the most part, they smiled at each other, then nodded to me in reply, their smiles lingering. I could tell it was weird to have a white man in this area, but liked the unguarded responses of the children. "If me being here is this abnormal," I thought, "then it's probably exactly where I belong."

Mr. Joe was the first member to arrive, followed shortly by another man I assumed was also a deacon. They immediately started setting up for the prayer service. I wanted to jump out and help, but I'd received a call from my supervisor, Jamie Cambetta, a fellow believer and a good man. We talked for almost 20 minutes while I felt like an albino rhino at the zoo, just sitting there while they did all the work. Utilizing the peace God had amply supplied moments ago, I brushed off my presumptive anxiety and paid attention to the work at hand.

After we wrapped up our call, I said a quick prayer for continued peace. As I exited my vehicle and approached the men doing the bulk of the pre-service work, Mr. Joe greeted me. His warm reception was a co-sign of sorts: I didn't have any credibility with the group, so he lent me some of his. I smiled and shook hands with a few people, but the man who stood out was Mr. June, a fellow deacon. If Mr. Joe was warm, this man was the surface of the sun! I don't know what Mr. Joe told him about me between our earlier meeting and my arrival at the prayer service, but it must have been good. Mr. June seemed legitimately thrilled to have me there. I wasn't expecting rudeness by any means, but this level of enthusiasm made an introduction feel like a homecoming.

Much like Mr. Joe's expression of brotherhood hours before, Mr. June's excitement empowered me to believe I was on the right track. After all, if these statesmen of the church, who had undoubtedly seen terrible racism during their 80-some-odd years of life in the deep South, were happy to have me, then my fears of offending God's hurting kids with my mere presence were probably unfounded. It almost seemed like the opposite was true. Maybe showing up was a ministry in itself. I wasn't sure and didn't want to assume, but my peace was intact and my courage was rising.

Most of the equipment had been unloaded, but we

tackled the remaining chores together. Right before finishing, I noticed one of the trucks had a low tire. Since I had an air compressor in my SUV, I offered to fill it back up. Immediately the men seemed a little ill at ease. Maybe it was because I was a guest. Maybe they weren't familiar with portable air compressors (the best $40 you'll ever spend, especially if you drive like me). I got the feeling it was because I was an unknown white man offering to do manual labor for them in my business casual attire. I couldn't be sure, but I was determined to fill that tire and any other with air, just in case it was the latter. "That'll have to wait until later—service is starting in a few minutes," was Mr. Joe's concluding verdict. With that, we all filed into the large store front.

There were forty or so metal folding chairs being set up by women and children next to a 6" tall stage in the otherwise empty 7,000 square foot room. Mr. Joe and Mr. June were occupied with some deaconly business, so I was left to amble around without my co-signing chaperones. Sans their covering, I was once again noticeably unlike everyone else in attendance. One lady asked if I owned the building. Another asked if I was a reporter. Up to that point, people had assumed I was a cop, a real estate owner, and a journalist. Obviously, the thought of a white man simply showing up as a fellow believer was preposterous. My response was to smile and let them know I invited myself when Mr. Joe told me about the service. Everyone was very polite, but the tune was noticeably awkward, even though the mood in the room was painfully mournful.

Right before the service began, Mr. Joe introduced me to the pastor of St. Mary's, Kyle Sylvester. As we shook hands, he introduced himself by his first name without title or ceremony. I loved that. While some may think it's disrespectful, I call everyone by their first name (unless they are older, then it's Mr. or Ms.). Jesus warned against calling people by their titles, and leaders who demand that "respect" are not normally worthy of it in my experience (Matthew 23). Any time anyone's ever addressed me as "pastor," I politely tell them, "My Mama named me Wes, so let's go with that." Not to belabor the point, but calling people by their role in ministry is actually a reduction of their value. God always calls people by name, because a parent doesn't address their child by their title. Our value as his kids is much higher than our value as his servants.

I realized Kyle was my age and very tired. As I learned later in the evening, he'd received hundreds of calls, texts, and emails in the last week. He had been dealing with innumerable officials, insurance adjusters, reporters, politicians, etc. for the last nine days. Not to mention someone had just burned down his church. He looked strong, but he had to be reeling from the insanity of his situation. I felt as though Kyle was very measured in his approach to me. In no way was he discourteous, but he had the bearing of a shepherd protecting his flock from a potential intruder. Once again, Mr. Joe was pulled away, leaving Kyle and I to continue our conversation alone. He was matter of fact as he asked me a very polite but direct question. Why are you here?

I said, "I had to do something. I read about the burnings and I couldn't do nothing." That answer seemed to suffice, so we moved on. I didn't know it, but my response did more than satisfy the pastor's question.

CHAPTER SIXTEEN

Redefining Service

Service to others is the rent you pay for your room here on earth.

— MUHAMMAD ALI

LIKE MOST CHURCH SERVICES, this one started with praise and worship music. Because it was a prayer service, they only sang one song: "Make Me a Servant One More Time." The lyrics floored me. Instead of singing a song about being comforted in affliction or justice for the faithful, they sang a song about sacrifice. Although the room was hardly set up for acoustic excellence, the spirit of the people connecting to their Father powerfully emphasized the presence of God in our midst. I was brought to tears almost immediately. Normally, I prefer thought-provoking lyrics in worship music, but this simple anthem couldn't have been more beautiful or impactful.

One of the most common stereotypes about black people in the South is that they love to play the "victim card." Many people believe that if there's even a hint of racial injustice in a situation, some black person somewhere will be offended and go on a tirade about 400 years of oppression. It probably is safe to say there are sensationalists who have made careers out of going from tragedy to tragedy, making big speeches and fleecing flocks to fill their own bank accounts. Nevertheless, the existence of a counterfeit doesn't render the authentic as worthless. These people had every reason to feel victimized, because they were! And yet they chose to ask the Lord for the honor of being a servant one more time.

Shortly after the music, Kyle asked for prayer requests. Roughly a dozen such requests were made, and each one was prayed over individually and by the name attached to the request. It was a very intimate time. I'd never seen a community that size so tightly knit and comfortable with each other. Amazingly, they even seemed comfortable with me in the room once the service started. In the presence of the Lord, we're all comfortable in our own skin. Next, Kyle asked if anyone wanted to come forward and share what was on their heart regarding the traumatic events they were enduring. While several people came forward, one woman's story hit me the hardest. Her family had been part of the church for generations, and her husband was a local firefighter. The day the church was burned they had been up in the early hours of the morning, feeling uneasy and not knowing why. Then the call came over the radio and her husband flew out the door. Driving as fast as possible on the country back roads, he arrived in time to see the church of his youth engulfed in flames. She mentioned her own frustration and anger towards the cowards who set fire to their church in the middle of the night, but it was the pain in her husband's eyes that caused her the most suffering. While everyone was being attacked by shame and sorrow, he was wrestling with the added guilt of thinking he should have done more to save their sanctuary. Her vulnerability with such troubling emotions was both inspirational and heartbreaking.

I guess that's why most churches don't bother with deep transparency. There's no comfortable little Christian box to put those kinds of feelings into. However, if we refuse to deal with our broken hearts and wounded souls within the safe confines of our family of faith, then we will never deal with them. Rather, eventually they will deal with us. I don't know how many church scandals we have to endure before we realize this level of openness isn't just a good idea during times of strife, but vital as part of our regular Christian community. If we can't be safe in a room full of people who openly admit they are worthless without their Savior, then where will we ever be safe?

As this part of the service came to a close, Kyle spoke about forgiveness and restoration. His leadership was beyond impressive. He affirmed pain, while refusing self-pity. He comforted doubt, but encouraged faith. He sympathized with anger, then instructed his people to forgive and trust the Lord for justice. Many of the congregants had freely expressed difficult emotions, and he was always right there to nod in agreement or bracket their statements with scripture if necessary. Honestly, it felt more like an expertly handled family counseling session than a church service at times. Strangely, even though this is exactly what I feared, I didn't feel as though I was hindering anyone's ability to honestly process their pain. I was awash in the beauty of the service. It's funny, we use that term "service" even though our church services are often more like church productions. This was no production—this was service. Service to the Lord, and service from the Lord to his beloved. The resolve and faithfulness of this family for their God still brings me to tears every time I remember that night. I was deeply humbled and blessed just to be present.

It's been a year since that fateful night, and I still don't know what was on Kyle Sylvester's mind as he started bringing the service to a close. He didn't seem flustered, but you could tell there was something lingering on his mind. He had brought several people up to the podium to speak, and was introducing the last person to share that night when it occurred to me every member of the church had already spoken or had been given a chance to speak. Was he about to bring someone up who hadn't volunteered? That seemed odd. Certainly, he wouldn't put someone on the spot like that... These thoughts had me zoned out for a few seconds as I scanned the room, so I didn't truly hear what he was saying. I only caught the last part: "This brother knows I can't let him leave without sharing why he came tonight. Wes, will you come on up and share?" A deer in the headlights has more composure than I had as he extended the microphone in my direction.

I whole-heartedly believe America can heal racial wounds, but it won't happen until we begin to understand that our most terrifying moments reflect the worst aspect of your everyday life.

— WES BROUSSARD

CHAPTER SEVENTEEN

Faith is Spelled R-I-S-K

Understanding waits on the other side of risk.

— SUZANNE WAGNER

An apology is like laughter: there are very few rules and it's good for the soul.

IT'S possible I was the only person in the room who didn't know he was introducing me, but I was honestly completely oblivious. Seeing my eyes widen to the point of absurdity, Kyle smiled warmly and told me it wasn't necessary for me to have "three points and a poem" (preacher talk for an established sermon at the ready just in case). He simply wanted me to share my heart. I knew it was God. I knew this was what he wanted from the first moment at that random gas station on I-10. This was the price and the payment for my "yes." I had the grace to embrace the moment, but my voice was shaking and my eyes were wet. The weight of decades of preparation, a scorching desire for racial reconciliation, and a genuine love for these amazing people were a gentle yoke on my soul. It was time to say what I knew God wanted me to share, but it was so irregular... so ungrounded. It didn't even make total sense to me, and I wasn't the one with a pile of ashes where my church had stood for 100-plus years.

I started by introducing myself, then mentioned The Best of Enemies. I shared what I'd learned from Anne Atwater and C.P. Ellis. Then I started to cry. I knew I had to go into the most broken part of my life in order to make God's message make sense. As I tried to compose myself, choking back racking robs, a wave of support and love arose from the congregation. They knew I needed their help and didn't hesitate to provide it. Finally, I started, "Last year, my wife of twelve years divorced me. She isn't a bad person, but she is definitely not a fan of mine." The first sentence produced empathic groans; the second brought a ripple of authentic laughter. I will not go into the details of my divorce here, because I don't want to dishonor anyone. Suffice it to say, it was a divorce—it was awful for everyone involved. "The worst part is the feeling of total helplessness," I continued. "I'm a big white man. I've never felt helpless a day in my life, until this last year. I can't stand it. I miss my children. I miss their faces and their laughs. Partial custody is killing me." Again, I started to sob uncontrollably. Again, they uplifted and consoled me. Their empathy for me, given what they were currently enduring and the fact that I was a total stranger, was unbelievable.

Catching my breath, I continued; "Being in the theater to see that movie, while I read an article about your church being burned down, was no accident. I never —and I mean never—have anything to do with the news media. That must have been the first news article I've read in... I couldn't tell you how many years. Then, during the film, the Lord was showing me how helpless I'd felt for the last year, and how that helplessness and fear are the reality for many people in this country every day. How, for the first time, I could genuinely relate to what it's like to have almost no power in a situation. To be assumed guilty of heinous crimes, even though there was no factual evidence to support the accusations. To have people sneer at me and even recoil from me when I tried to shake their hands. Some of those people I'd known for 20 years. Some of them helped lead me to Christ. Yet, based on rumors alone, I was assumed guilty and cast aside as worthless. All of a sudden, I went from a brother in Christ and a trusted minister to something less than a man, even though none of those people ever bothered to speak to me or get my side of the story. My side was irrelevant. I was irrelevant."

At this point in my little speech, I felt the mood shifting from curiosity and empathy to cautious expectation. Despite the recent attacks, these believers were ready to receive, if I was ready to trust God and risk a total disaster. I leaned in. "I honestly don't know how much good it will do, but I believe God brought me here tonight for one main reason: to apologize to you on behalf of white America." I think it's safe to say, the congregation of St. Mary's wasn't expecting that. After pausing for a moment, I added, "Until last year, I'd never known what it was like to be assumed guilty, to be looked at like a threat or worse without just cause. I'd been the only white kid on black basketball teams. I'd lived as the only white family on a black street. I'd mentored dozens of inmates in a prison whose population was over 70% black men. I'd worked in communities so disenfranchised that huge portions of the walls of their trailer homes were torn down, leaving black mothers and their children exposed to the elements year-round. I'd traveled to Africa to minister in extremely remote parts of Ethiopia, where the locals had killed the first white people they'd ever seen, around the same time your church was being planted. I was considered to be an especially "woke" white person (i.e. sensitive and open-minded to issues of systematic racial oppression). Still, none of that prepared me to walk a mile in your shoes. And it probably wasn't even a whole mile, but it felt like it to me. I'm so sorry. It isn't fair. You shouldn't have to live with that pain and the crippling shame that comes with it. I'm so, so sorry. Please accept my apology for what it's like to be black in America."

Never doubt that a small group of thoughtful, committed citizens can change the world; indeed, it's the only thing that ever has.

— MARGARET MEAD

CHAPTER EIGHTEEN

Understanding Breeds Wisdom

If you only hear one side of the story, you have no understanding at all.

— CHINUA ACHEBE

THERE WAS a general murmur of what I sincerely hoped was something close to healing among the forty other souls in the room. Encouraged by their tacit approval, I moved on to my conclusion: "I believe most well-meaning white people simply don't know how to relate to what the average black person in America is going through. It's not that they don't care or can't sense something is off—they do. We do. It's just that we don't get it. I don't mean to sound blithe and simplistic, but it's true. We don't live our lives with that fear. However, we do have moments and seasons that drive us to our knees. It's those experiences that have brought me here. I whole-heartedly believe America can heal racial wounds, but it won't happen until we begin to understand that our most terrifying moments reflect the worst aspect of your everyday life."

Honestly, I don't have a recording from that night and the emotions of the day were overwhelming, so I'm sure that's an imperfect recollection. Nevertheless, that's the lion's share of what God put on my heart to say. Everything after that was a blur until we left the building. I remember laughter and warm embraces as we picked up the chairs and sound equipment. Every Wednesday, two lovely ladies provide to-go dinners for the Bible study attendees and their children in order to soften the burden of feeding families so close to bedtime. Now, the hard part was over. I'd risked rubbing salt in the wounds of God's beloved, because I trusted him it wouldn't be salt but healing balm. By all accounts, the risk was well worth it.

As soon as everyone finished hugging and handshaking, I made sure I aired up that low tire that had been mentioned before the service. Wrapping up, Kyle looked at me and said, "I think you needed that, too." I saw his pastor's eyes look at me like I was one of his sacred flock. I replied, "Oh, yes, like you wouldn't believe."

As Providence would have it, a mutual friend of ours, Floyd Prescott, who I'd ministered with years before, approached seemingly out of nowhere. I knew he lived in the area, but didn't know he held services nearby. It was a surprising and welcomed reunion. Kyle, Floyd, and I talked for a few minutes until I got a text from Stanley, one of the parishioners who had asked for my number. I said my final goodbyes and started the drive home with Stanley in my ear and a relieved and exhilarated smile on my face. We talked for quite a while. Having listened to me talk about the pain and brokenness of my divorce, Stanley wanted to encourage me with his testimony. He did just that. All in all, it was a good night filled with God's kids loving each other. There was still an overwhelming amount of justice, reconciliation, and healing left undone; nevertheless, risks were taken all around, and God proved himself a good Father yet again.

They cannot touch your real power, because they aren't the ones who gave it to you. God, who is true power, has empowered you far beyond the reach of others' hatred.

— WES BROUSSARD

SECTION FOUR: HOW TO WIN

We will work together to remove the external threats and lies that come against this truth, but only you can ingratiate this reality into your culture and future generations.

— WES BROUSSARD

CHAPTER NINETEEN

Hail to the Victors

Somehow I won in a game of tug of war with the sun, and discovered I'd been underestimating the strength of my own light for entirely too long.

— CURTIS TYRONE JONES

I'VE STAYED in contact with Brother Lea and Stanley for the last year. My family and I have attended a few services at St. Mary's, too. Last weekend, we went to Kyle's book signing. I can't wait to dive into his latest project, Ram in the Bush. It's been a beautiful blessing. Soon, they will open their fellowship hall, which will serve as their sanctuary until the construction of their new church is complete. I have listened to many hours of Kyle's sermons and podcasts during the quarantine. He has faced the evolving issues of our time head on—police brutality, peaceful protests, riots—but he's always reached for the love, power, and wisdom of God. It's been said, "You can't demote your theology to the level of your worst experiences." That means God is God. He is perfect love and justice, even when our lives are seemingly filled with hate and injustice.

I learned a very important lesson that night at St. Mary's: no one is helpless. When they opened the service with "Make Me a Servant One More Time," it was a clarion call that this beautiful body of believers was not going to back down on the goodness and love of God, no matter what evil attacked them. God is God. Our entire reality hinges on who we are to him and who he is to us. No, they couldn't stop the white supremacist who was eventually arrested for destroying these churches, but they did stop his hate from infecting their faith. They prayed for him, truly crying out to God for their terrorist's salvation. Kyle even said the man (who was also a sheriff's deputy's son) was no more guilty than any one of the members of St. Mary's, because without the blood of Jesus we are all equally condemned. This message is clear in Scripture, but believing it under the circumstances faced by St. Mary's congregation taught me just how powerful these "victims" truly were.

In recent years, I've experienced more hate and injustice than I ever thought possible. It's been a very rough ride. One friend, Gary Spears, told me, "Wes, you've died well." That's probably the best compliment I've ever received. My closest friend, Chris Thomas, has told me on multiple occasions, "I couldn't have survived what you went through. There's no way. I'd be dead or in jail." Another dear friend, Jonathon Louis, said, "You've taken away my ability to say 'No' to God. I've seen you say 'Yes' to him so many times and in the face of so much pain— you've taken away my excuses."

I wish I could tell you I'm out of that season, but it continues to ramble around my life like a rat in the walls of my soul. The pain and anger and fear are overwhelming at times, especially when I'm alone in the middle of the night. About a month ago, while I was wallowing around in genuine pain and ridiculous self-pity, God spoke to me very directly. If you have ever had him speak to you very directly, you know what I mean. There's no guessing, complaining, or countering. There's only receiving and being very still. He said,

No one is powerless, because I have given everyone the power to reject me.

In that moment, I knew I was always powerful, even

though injustice made me feel like a helpless victim. The very Creator of power, choice, sex, music, love, wonder has given each of us the most daring and preposterous power in the cosmos: the power to reject or accept him. Yes, people can victimize us. Still, the higher reality, the greater truth St. Mary's exhibited for me that night and in every encounter since, is that we are born with more power than we'll ever need. If we have the power to deny God, after all Jesus did for us on the cross, then why don't we use that same power to dismiss lies, attacks, and fear? I'm not saying this is always easy, but I am saying there's powerful truth in the point God made to me that night. This is not an easy truth for me to swallow at times, especially when the injustices and hate are raw, but God is God. I don't get to demote him or myself based on my worst experiences, especially if I'm ever going to be whole, let alone leave a powerful spiritual inheritance for my children. His truth is how we change the world.

To my black readers: You are powerful. Yes, people have victimized you for simply being born with darker skin. That's an awful reality I'll never understand. Still, they cannot touch your real power, because they aren't the ones who gave it to you. God, who is true power, has empowered you far beyond the reach of others' hatred. Embrace the role of the powerful son and daughter. Teach your children how beautiful and powerful they are. We will work together to remove the external threats and lies that come against this truth, but only you can ingratiate this reality into your culture and future generations.

Racism must be taught; so, we are always only one generation away from toppling this sadistic evil in our midst.

— WES BROUSSARD

CHAPTER TWENTY

Finally

Washing one's hands of the conflict between the powerful and the powerless means to side with the powerful, not to be neutral.

— PAULO FREIRE

I STARTED WRITING this book on January 1st, 2020, and had been chipping away with moderate success until the murders of Ahmad Asbury, Breonna Taylor, and George Floyd. Once again, our nation erupted into a racially supercharged cacophony of anger, fear, and sorrow. Writing my little book seemed almost vain in the midst of those events. All of this has happened before, but this time there were a few new wrinkles worth mentioning. First of all, officers of the law have been fired and even charged with murder. To my knowledge, that's never happened before, especially not on so large and visible a stage. Also, enormous numbers of white people have joined the movement, both on social media and in the streets of America. This isn't a single night of rage-induced agony or agony-induced rage. There are millions of Americans and scores of powerful influencers who are forcefully wrestling with this evil, hoping to enact real change. I don't know why it has taken so long, but I'm relieved to see change happening now.

Some of my white friends can't seem to understand the emotions and logic behind the Black Lives Matter movement. A very easy first step to understanding would be to realize that without this movement, these officers would still be patrolling the streets of their respective cities. When you choke somebody out with your knee on their neck for just short of nine minutes, it's wildly obvious you should not be entrusted with the authority that comes with being a police officer. When you realize that same officer had eighteen other incidents on his record, but was still training new officers on the very day he murdered George Floyd, you begin to understand the urgency of the movement.

The BLM movement is admirable and has my full

support. I know there are differences between the political agenda and social agenda. Still, chipping away at the fringe of a group in order to dismiss their movement entirely is not in keeping with Christian values. People have persecuted Christians for eons using the same logic. It's easy to critique a group of people, especially when they are reacting in visceral pain. However, as believers, we were not given the ministry of "easy"; we were given the ministry of reconciliation. That's why so many younger, white Americans have jumped at the opportunity to support this movement. They want to be part of the reconciliation, the termination of injustice, the healing of generational and national wounds. That's also why this particular wave will reach the shore of realization—we're not going to stop until America is made whole.

Stephen Covey said it best: "Seek first to understand, then to be understood." As hundreds of millions of Americans watch riots and peaceful protests alike unfold on their screens each night, the talking heads and pundits race around, frantically searching for a way to control influence over us so they can continue to make money off of us. The easiest way to do that is to pit us against one another. They have made untold trillions doing just that. If you want to continue to fund and empower these ungodly powers, then keep closing your eyes and ears to the pain of your neighbor. Go ahead, keep ignoring any narrative that doesn't fit perfectly into your world view. But you will be manipulated and robbed. On the other hand, if you want to be part of the solution, then empathize with those who've been wronged, reach out to people who don't look like you in your community, and begin to build bridges of unity within your spheres of influence.

My prayer is that we would see this movement as human, which means it deserves the same dignity that's given to any image-bearer of God, and the same grace for mistakes. If nothing else, for the first time in US history, there are consequences for killing these American citizens. It disturbs and wounds me that this is not celebrated at every level, especially in the church.

CHAPTER TWENTY-ONE

One Generation Away

He who does not understand your silence will probably not understand your words.

— ELBERT HUBBARD

FOR MY WHITE READERS, please keep in mind the events I've outlined throughout this book didn't happen in the convenient vacuum of history. They happened to friends and heroes of mine not that long along. Also, these Americans are not alone in their experiences; but in many ways, the black community is very much alone in dealing with this unbridled hate. It's not because all white people are unsympathetic. No, it's because most white people don't have a single close black friend, so they've never been entrusted with these horror stories. Before you get offended by that statement, if you are the white person that has to count your black friends, it's safe to say you are who I'm talking about. I get it. Most of my friends are white, too. I'm not talking about being the lone "woke" white person at an all black cookout just for the sake of being anti-racists. I've known white men who would only marry a black woman, because they wanted to fight racism - that's definitely not what I'm talking about either. I'm talking about facing the awkwardness and tension you feel when the black people you know are hurting, even when you don't personally understand their experience. Step in the gap for them. Set aside political agenda and be present with them in the pain. Be there as a balm, an olive branch, a friend.

Very, very recently, we have seen white people come out in droves to support black Americans, and it's beautiful. We need that desperately. However, being vocal on social media and attending protests cannot be the extent of our resolve. We must love our neighbors deeply enough to be included in their pain; otherwise, in the very near future, it will be too easy to dismiss these offenses as things of the past that black people should have gotten over by now. Until we become acquainted with someone's pain, we can't really understand it, let alone fight for the victims in any redemptive way. If you knew Carl and Reggie, you'd understand and you'd fight like hell for them and their families. If you'd seen a body of believers worship their hearts out while their church was still smoldering, you'd be honored and humbled to call yourself their friend and you'd pray they'd call you brother. If you had seen the look on Mr. Hank Williams's face when that punk kid called him a nigger, you'd fight through the tension to be there for him. I truly believe you would. Of course you would.

The good news is you have Carls and Reggies and Mr. Williamses and persecuted black churches in your life right now. Maybe you don't spend time with them, but you can. You should. Don't act weird. Just treat them like anyone else you would like to get to know better. Before long, you'll find yourself opened up to a reality you never knew existed, even though it was right in front of your nose. Still, as you learn about the differences in your American lives, understanding and empathy will be much more readily accessible. Ignorant judgements will fall away. Actual solutions and partnerships will be birthed. Paradigms will shift. Remember, racism must be taught; so, we are always only one generation away from toppling this sadistic evil in our midst. Be on the right side of history, so nobody's mother ever has to wake up to a cross in their front yard, or a congregation to their church on fire.

FOR THE SAKE OF CLARITY: BLUE PRINT

Stop setting goals. Goals are pure fantasy unless you have a specific plan to achieve them.

— STEPHEN COVEY

Normally, I wouldn't try to "gift wrap" the ending of a book, but I would hate for you to come to the end of this book without an actionable plan moving forward. Hopefully, the Lord has spoken to you as you read, because the development between you and God as it pertains to loving his kids is more important than any three-point plan I can provide. With that being said, here's my three-point plan:

1. Walk in Power

- We are more empowered by God than we are victimized by life.
- If we teach our children they are powerful, culture can be revolutionized in one generation.

2. Love Overrides Politics

- We must collaborate with groups based on the common ground of our faith and our value for life, instead of being divided by political arguments.
- We are citizens of Heaven before we are citizens of America or members of a particular political party.
- If the talking points of your political party are interfering with your love for your neighbor, then you are over-valuing politics and under-valuing God's family.
- This is very widely done on social media platforms, because we are more likely to have a knee-jerk response than a thoughtful response when we are alone and online.

3. Intimacy Leads to Empathy

- If you haven't been entrusted with someone's broken places, then it will be hard to empathize with them when controversial issues arise.
- Put in the light-duty work of growing in relationships with people of different backgrounds.
- A whole new world will open up to you. A world you've lived in all your life, and even contributed to, but didn't know existed. Once you peek behind this veil, everything will change.

From the beginning, the main point of this book has been to help moderate, conservative, white Christians realize we are living in the Matrix to a degree. We have been lulled into indifference, not because we are terrible people, but because the helplessness of our neighbors has always been a mystery to us. I sincerely hope this book has popped open the lid of this issue to allow you to look inside.

My dream is that you will take this newfound understanding and run with it. On this run, I know you will connect with your own St. Mary's Missionary Baptist Church. You will be rescued by your own Mr. Joe. You will befriend your own Carls and Reggies. You will honor and remember your own Mr. Keiths and Mr. Hanks. Fight for your neighbors. Love them well.

> *He has told you, O man, what is good; And what does the Lord require of you but to do justice, to love kindness, And to walk humbly with your God?*

> — MICAH 6:8, (NASB)

> *But he's already made it plain how to live, what to do, what God is looking for in men and women. It's quite simple: Do what is fair and just to your neighbor, be compassionate and loyal in your love, And don't take yourself too seriously— take God seriously.*

> — MICAH 6:8 (THE MESSAGE)

Like most Americans, when Wes Broussard was a child, he invented his own god without even knowing it. He spent years praying to and trying to obey this non-existent deity, until the day he met Jesus. Since that February night, Wes has truly experienced a new life. He graduated TM's Honor Academy two years later, then entered LSU as a religious studies major. Through nearly two decades of church leadership and five years as a prison pastor, Wes has learned that true ministry is loving the one in front of you well. His devotion to relational ministry and Biblical unity drive him as a pastor and reformer. Wes has six incredible children: Mariah, Eli, Canaan, Blaze, Wes Jr., and Zach.